# WELCOME TO BRITAIN

### Jimmie Hill
### Michael Lewis

**Language and Information
for the Foreign Visitor**

Language Teaching Publications
35 Church Road, Hove, BN3 2BE, England

**Acknowledgements**
Bob Stearn for information on page 56 from The International Student.

Punch for several cartoons.

Mike Gordon for cartoons on pp 25, 53.

▶    When you see this symbol, try to learn the language which comes after it. Try saying it aloud. Ask your teacher if you sound natural.

Printed by Commercial Colour Press, London E7, England.

# Contents

# 1 Enjoy your stay

## Britain is different

Britain is different from your own country. You will like some of the differences, and some you will not be so keen on. This is natural. The more you try to understand us, the more you will enjoy your stay – even when you don't agree with us! Here are some points to help you make the most of your stay.

## Are the British positive to visitors?

In some towns, especially on the south coast of England, there are very large numbers of students in the summer. Try to understand the problems of the local people – for example, getting to work in the morning when the buses are crowded. Try to imagine your own home town if there were thousands of foreign students!

## Are you in your teens?

If you are, look after yourself. Go around town with friends. If possible, try to make a British friend. Ask your school if they can put you in touch with a British person of your own age.

## Your first time in a British home?

If it is, make the most of it! Your host family is a valuable source of ideas and information about Britain and about English. Most British people love to talk about language and especially about the differences in accent between different parts of Britain. You can learn a lot from your host family.

## British food

We all like what we are used to. British food can be just as good as food anywhere else! Perhaps you are not too keen on British mealtimes. It is quite normal for British families to eat their evening meal as early as 5.30pm or 6pm. The advantage is that your whole evening is free. If this is very different from your country, try to understand!

# 1 *Enjoy your stay*

## Are the British polite?

The British are no more or less 'polite' than any other nation.
However, there are a few English words which are very important,
and if you do not use them, you will upset people and then you will
be upset. The most important words are:

**please    thank you    excuse me    sorry**

You can read more about these words on pages 66–68.

## What about your teacher?

If you are at a language school, this may be the first time you have
studied English in Britain with a British teacher. You may think that
the teaching is very different from your own school. Perhaps you
think the atmosphere is more (too?) relaxed. Language schools are
less formal. Most students come to Britain to improve their spoken
English. The best way to do that is in a more relaxed atmosphere.

## Crowded buses

British people like to think they know what is 'fair'. This is one of the
reasons they queue in straight lines! If they cannot get to work on
their normal bus because there are 200 students trying to get on
without queuing, try to understand if they don't seem as happy as
usual.

*"I keep telling you—in England
we **queue**!"*

# 2 Essential to know

If you have just arrived in Britain, here is some information which you may need immediately.

## Please

When you ask for something, say *please* at the end.
**A single to Victoria, please.**
**A packet of these, please.**

## Toilets

Public toilets may be called *Lavatories* or *Conveniences* on public signs. Outside it will say either *Gents* or *Gentlemen* and *Ladies*.
In the street, ask:
**Excuse me, can you tell me where the nearest toilet is, please.**
In someone's home, use:
**Could I use the loo/toilet, please.**

## Queuing

Queuing is normal in Britain. People will become very angry, and even rude, if you 'jump' the queue. If you go in front of someone by accident, say:
**Oh, I'm sorry. I didn't realise.**

## Groups

If you are on a language course in one of the popular towns in the south of England – where there are lots of foreign students – avoid walking around the town in large groups. Many elderly people become frightened if they have to walk on the road because the pavement is crowded with students. Think of your own home town if thousands of young British students walked around in large groups!

# 2 Essential to know

## Alcohol

Attitudes to alcohol are different in different countries. Attitudes in Britain are fairly relaxed. However, it is a serious crime to sell drink to anyone under the age of 18. If you are 18, but look younger, a barman in a pub may ask you to prove your age. Do not be angry about this. He is only doing his job.

## Telephones

You can use any public telephone in Britain to make an international call. There are two kinds of public telephone: those which take coins and those which take telephone cards. You can buy telephone cards from newsagents and any shop which has a sign on the window advertising them.

## 999

The emergency number for police, fire, and ambulance is 999.

## Problems

If you do not understand someone, say:

> **I'm sorry I don't understand. Could you speak more slowly, please. I'm a foreign student.**

If someone becomes angry because of something you have said, say:

> **I'm sorry. I don't speak English very well. I didn't mean to upset you.**

# 3 Arriving

## At your host family

Hello, you must be Maria. How do you do?

► **Hello, how do you do.**

Come in. Did you have a good journey?

► **Yes, it was fine, thanks.**

**How do you do** is used the first time you meet and mostly by older people. Reply **How do you do** or **Pleased to meet you.** Younger people use **Hello**.

Hello. Come in. You must be tired.

► **Hello. Yes, I'm sorry I'm so late. My plane was delayed, and then it took ages to get through Customs at Heathrow.**

Never mind. You're here now. Come and have a cup of tea.

► **Thank you very much.**

## At a guest house or hotel

Hello, do you have a reservation?

► **Yes, my name is** _____ .

Ah, yes. You're in room 24, on the second floor.
That's for two weeks, isn't it?

► **Yes, that's right. I leave on** _____ .

## Worth knowing

● It is normal to shake hands in Britain when you meet someone for the first time. It is not usual to kiss.

● It is not necessary to arrive with a present if you are a paying guest in a British home. On the other hand, your host family will be very impressed if you do!

● Use your host family's first names ONLY if they encourage you to.

# 3 Arriving

## First Questions

Here are some questions you may want to ask at the beginning of your stay:

## If you are with a host family

**When do you have breakfast/dinner?**
**Is it alright to have a shower?**
**Will I have my own key?**

## If you are in a guest house/hotel

**When does breakfast begin/end?**
**When is dinner?**
**Is the outside door locked at night?**
**How can I get in if I come home very late?**
**Do you have a public telephone?**

## General questions

**Can I walk to the school or should I take a bus?**
**How long will it take to walk there?**
**How long does it take to walk to the town centre?**
**Where can I change money today/tomorrow morning?**

## Practice

Write the questions to which these are the answers:

1._____

Certainly, but remember to put the curtain INSIDE before you turn the water on.

2._____

It's a good 25 minutes walk. I'd get the no. 44 bus if I were you.

3._____

Oh, don't worry about that. There's always someone at home.

# 4 Who are you?

## Who are you?

I'm Hiromi. I'm Japanese. I come from Osaka. This is my first visit to Britain. I'm on a course in Bournemouth. I'm staying for three weeks. I'm a student.

My name's Jonas. I'm Swedish. I come from Uppsala. I'm 20. I've been to Britain twice before. I'm on a course in Cambridge. I'm very interested in history.

I'm Pilar. I'm Spanish. I come from Seville. That's in the south of Spain. I'm on a two week course in Eastbourne. I love lying on the beach, swimming and sunbathing. I'm a tour guide.

I'm Ricardo. I'm Italian and I come from Turin. I am at university, but I cannot speak English very well. I'm on a course for six weeks. I want to become a journalist. That is why I need good English.

## Worth knowing

● Notice these questions:
**Where do you come from?** – I come from Japan.
**Whereabouts in Japan?** – From Osaka.
**Whereabouts** = where exactly?

● Notice we use the present simple to say:
**I come** from Italy. **I live** in Turin.
We use the present continuous to say:
**I'm staying** here in Eastbourne for three weeks.

● When you give your job, you say **I'm a** guide/**I'm a** teacher.

# 4 Who are you?

## Talk about yourself

What's your name?

▶ **I'm _____. My surname is _____.**

**That's spelt _____. My friends call me**

**_____.**

Where are you from?

▶ **I'm from _____, from a town called _____.**

**It's in the _____ of _____.**

How long is your course?

▶ **I'm on a _____-week course at the _____ school.**

What do you do?

▶ **At the moment I'm a _____. I work/study _____.**

Have you been to Britain before?

▶ **Yes, I was here in _____. I was in _____.**

**(No, this is my first visit.)**

What are you interested in?

▶ **The thing I am most interested in is _____.**

Why is learning English important to you?

▶ _____

# 5 Breakfast

## Information

● Nowadays most British people have a 'continental-type' breakfast:

**cereal and/or fruit juice**
**tea or coffee with toast, bread, or a roll**
**butter and marmalade (orange jam)**

If you are in a guest house, hotel, or living with a host family, you will be offered the choice of a continental breakfast or a 'full English' breakfast. This includes the continental breakfast PLUS:

**fried bacon**
**fried, boiled, or scrambled egg**
**fried mushrooms**
**fried tomatoes**
**fried sausages**

● Sometimes the full English breakfast is called a 'cooked breakfast'. If you are in a hotel, you may also be offered kippers. (Scottish smoked herring)

● If you are living with a host family, they may ask you on your first night what kind of breakfast you would like.

## When you arrive for breakfast

Good morning, did you sleep well?

▶ **Yes thank you, very well.**

You do not need to say more. The question means, 'Was everything alright in your room.' You do NOT ask your host if he/she slept well!

# 5 *Breakfast*

## What would you like?

Decide what you would like for breakfast from this list:

| | | | | | |
|---|---|---|---|---|---|
| cornflakes | ___ | muesli | ___ | grapefruit | ___ |
| orange juice | ___ | tea | ___ | white coffee | ___ |
| black coffee | ___ | milk | ___ | white bread | ___ |
| brown bread | ___ | toast | ___ | rolls | ___ |
| butter | ___ | marmalade | ___ | a boiled egg | ___ |
| a fried egg | ___ | bacon | ___ | scrambled egg | ___ |
| fried mushrooms | ___ | sausages | ___ | fried tomatoes | ___ |
| a kipper | ___ | | | | |

If you expect cheese at breakfast, you may have to ask for it specially.

## Questions

How do you like your coffee?

▶ **Black/white, please.**

Do you take milk in your tea?

▶ **Yes please/No thank you.**

Do not use **Yes** or **No** alone in your answer. They can sound aggressive. You will hear people say **Please** on its own to mean **Yes please.**

Would you like an egg?

▶ **Yes please/No thank you.**

Are you sure you wouldn't like one?

▶ **Yes, quite sure. I'm afraid I'm not very keen on eggs.**

# 6 Greetings

## Hello, how are you?

In Britain, friendly people start conversations with friends by saying, **Hello, how are you**. Practise this pattern:

**Hello, how are you?**

| | | |
|---|---|---|
| Fine | thanks. | And you? |
| Very well | thank you. | |
| Not too bad | | |

Remember, this is not a question about your health so (except to a very close friend) you do not reply, for example, *I've got a cold*, or *I've got a headache*.

Use the pattern above even if you are not very well. That is because it is part of the greeting, not a question about your health. If you are not very well and want to mention it you usually say later in the conversation:

**As a matter of fact I've got** (a bit of a cold/a bad throat.)

## Regards (when leaving)

**Give my regards to ....
Tell .... I was asking about him/her.
Remember me to ....
Oh, (thank you) I'll do that.**

You report this with:

**.... sent his/her regards.
.... asked to be remembered to you.
Oh, thank you. Give him/her my regards when you see him/her.**

## On someone's birthday

Say:   **Happy Birthday** or **Many Happy Returns**
Reply: **Thank you.**

# 6 Greetings

## On 1st January (and just after)

Say: **Happy New Year**
Reply: **Thank you. The same to you.**

## When someone is going away

Say: **Have a good holiday/trip**, or **Safe journey**.
Reply: **Thank you**.

Remember that **journey** refers only to the travelling. **Trip** refers to all the travelling and your stay.

## To congratulate someone

Say: **Congratulations!**
Reply: **Thank you**.

This is used when someone has got engaged, got married, passed an examination, passed a driving test, got promotion, had a baby.
**Congratulations** is also used when someone is celebrating a special birthday. The most important birthdays for British people are 18, 21, 70, 80 etc. Special wedding anniversaries are 25th(Silver) and 50th(Golden).

What are the special birthdays and anniversaries in your country?

*"Greetings, Earthman."*

# 7 Your host family 1

## Asking if you can do something

▶ **Do you mind if I have a shower every morning?**
▶ **Would you mind if I had a shower every morning?**

Notice with **Do you mind** – the verb is in the present – **have**. With **Would you mind** – the verb is in the past – *had*. These are very similar in meaning. The question with *would* is a little more formal, and, depending on the person you are speaking to, more polite.

Here are other ways of asking if you can do something:

**Is it all right if I bring a friend round?**
**Would it be all right if I had dinner later tomorrow?**
**May I use the phone for a local call, please?**
**When's the best time for me to have a bath/shower?**

## Practice

Use these different ways to ask if you can do the following:

1. wash a few clothes

   _____

2. dry some socks in the bathroom

   _____

3. have an early dinner tomorrow

   _____

4. put the light on

   _____

5. look at the newspaper

   _____

6. watch the tennis

   _____

7. borrow a hairdryer

   _____

8. make a reversed charge phone call

   _____

# 7 Your host family 1

## When you need something

| | |
|---|---|
| **Do you think I could**<br>**I wonder if I could** | have another blanket/pillow.<br>borrow a pair of scissors.<br>use the iron.<br>have a few more coat hangers.<br>have some extra heating in my room.<br>borrow the telephone directory. |

| | |
|---|---|
| **Sorry, but could you show me** | where I can use my razor, please.<br>how to turn on the shower, please. |

## Telling your host of a problem

| | |
|---|---|
| **I'm very sorry but** | I think I've lost my key.<br>I've spilt my coffee.<br>I think I've broken the lamp. |

▶ **I'm really very sorry...I would like to pay for it.**
  Oh, don't worry. It's all right.

▶ **No, really, I'd be happier if you let me pay.**
  No, really. It's quite all right. These things happen.

▶ **Oh, I am sorry.**

## When you are going to be late home

▶ **Oh, by the way,** I won't be in until quite late this evening.

▶ **Oh, by the way,** I may be a bit late this evening, **please don't wait up for me.**

## Practice

What do you say in these situations:

1. You want to have a shower after dinner this evening.
2. You want to wash some shirts.
3. You want to ring the railway station.
4. You want to borrow some black shoe polish.
5. You want to borrow a comb.
6. You have broken a glass in your room.
7. You are going on a trip and will not get back till 1 am.
8. You think you have broken the hot water tap in the bathroom.

# 8 Your host family 2

## Offering to help

▶ **Can I do anything?**
▶ **Can I give you a hand with that?**
▶ **Let me...**
When it is clear what you are offering to do – for example, lay the table, dry the dishes etc.

▶ **Would you like me to** | post it for you?
| call in and pick it up for you?
| run down to the shops for you?

## Warning someone

▶ **Mind (your glass)!**
▶ **Watch out!**
▶ **Be careful!** | There's a wasp (on your collar).
| There's a glass under your chair.

## Saying thank you

For something small:
▶ **Thanks.**     or   **Thanks very much.**
▶ **Thank you.**  or   **Thank you very much.**

For something more important:
▶ **Thank you VERY much.** | **That WAS kind of you.**
| **I'm VERY grateful.**

Notice that one word is given very heavy stress. Make sure you can say these so that you sound really grateful.

Finally, at the end of your stay:
▶ **Thank you very much for looking after me. I've really enjoyed staying with you.**

# 8 Your host family 2

## An important custom

If you are sitting in a British home and you want to leave the room for any reason, your host will expect you to say where you are going – even if it is obvious. If you leave the room without explaining, people will think you are ill or upset for some reason.
If you listen to your host family, you will almost certainly notice that they always say where they are going when they leave the room – even if they don't know they do it!

Here are some of the things you may want to say:

▶ **Would you excuse me,**    I think I'd better go and do my homework.
       I'm just going to write a few postcards.

Even if you are just going to the toilet, you say something:

▶ **Excuse me a moment.**
▶ **Excuse me, I'm just going upstairs.**
▶ **Excuse me, I'll just go you-know-where.**

Try to collect other phrases as you listen.

## Practice

What do you say in these situations:

1. There's an insect on your host's lettuce.

2. You have just borrowed a pen.

3. Your host has just taken you for a drive in the country.

4. You want to go to your room. You are very tired.

5. You are in the sitting-room. You want to go to the toilet.

6. You want to help do the dishes after a lovely meal.

7. Your host is on the point of sitting on a newspaper. There's a plate underneath it!

8. Your host is going to cut the grass. You want to help.

19

# 9 Pubs

## Information

**You must understand this**

You are not allowed to buy alcohol unless you are 18.

You may only go into a British pub before you are 18, if you are with an adult.

Pubs in Britain are not the same as pubs in your country. They are not cafes. If you are with a British friend who buys you a drink, you should offer to buy the next one.

It is unusual for each person in a group to order his/her own drink individually. It is more common for one person to order for everyone.

## Basic dialogue

Offer: **What would you like to drink?**

Reply: **I'll have (half a pint of bitter), please.**

Note: *What do you want to drink* is more informal and can sound less friendly to someone you do not know very well.

## Eating and Drinking

● There are five common different kinds of draught beer:

| | |
|---|---|
| **Lager** | – a light coloured beer, similar to German or Scandinavian beer |
| **Bitter** | – darker in colour, the most 'ordinary' English beer (called 'Heavy' in Scotland) |
| **Mild** | – a darker sweeter beer, less popular than bitter |
| **Guinness** | – the famous Irish beer, black in colour with a creamy 'head' to it, a kind of dark stout |

**Non-alcoholic** or **low-alcohol beer** is usually sold by name. If you ask for a low-alcohol beer, the bar staff will tell you what they have.

● Most pub beer is sold on draught. You can see the names of each one available on the pumps at the bar. You order them by the pint or half-pint:

| | | | | |
|---|---|---|---|---|
| A | pint | of | bitter | please. |
| | half-pint | | lager | |
| | | | mild | |

# 9 Pubs

- There are also many beers which are sold in bottles. You ask for them by name:

  **A bottle of (Tetley's, Ruddles), please.**

- Here is how to ask for other alcoholic drinks:

  **a scotch**        **a scotch and soda**
  **a dry martini**    **a campari soda**
  **a glass of white/red wine**

- Here are the commonest non-alcoholic drinks:

  **a low or non-alcoholic beer**
  **an orange juice**    **a grapefruit juice**
  **a ginger ale**       **a tonic water**
  **a bottle of ginger beer**

- You may also want to ask for the following:

  **A packet of peanuts**

If you want potato crisps, ask for the flavour:

| **A packet of** | **cheese and onion**<br>**roast chicken**<br>**salt and vinegar**<br>**plain** | **crisps, please.** |
|---|---|---|

- Some pubs serve coffee at lunchtime – others serve it all day.

## Pub Lunch

Most pubs serve snacks at lunchtime. Some serve excellent hot meals. Some only serve sandwiches. There are no rules for this. Every pub is different.

Can you pair up the popular British dishes on the left with the explanations on the right:

1. Ploughman's Lunch
2. Shepherd's Pie
3. Bangers and Mash
4. Cornish Pasty
5. Steak and Kidney Pie

a. sausages with potatoes
b. meat baked under pastry
c. meat and vegetable in pastry
d. cheese, pickles, and bread
e. minced meat covered with mashed potato

| 1 | 2 | 3 | 4 | 5 |
|---|---|---|---|---|
|   |   |   |   |   |

# 10 *Cafe Lunch*

## Information

● British cafes usually only serve soft (non-alcoholic) drinks.

● If you are having a meal in a cafe, you will be offered tea or coffee at the same time.

● You can expect the following on a typical menu:

Soup – tomato, chicken

Cod and chips
Haddock and chips
Huss and chips
Plaice and chips
Scampi and chips
Chicken and chips
Hamburger, beans and chips
Sausage, egg, and chips
Steak pie, peas, and chips
Sausage roll, beans, and chips
Pasty, beans, and chips
Salads – ham, chicken

Ice cream, apple tart
Pot of tea
Coffee
Soft drinks
Bread and butter

● If you have been served by a waiter or waitress and you want to pay, ask:

▶ **Could I pay now, please.**

▶ **Could I have the bill, please.**

▶ **The bill, please.**

Remember that **please** is very important.

# 10 Cafe Lunch

## Ordering

Fill in what you would like from the menu opposite:

Waiter: Now, are you ready to order?

You: **Yes, I think I'll start with** _____ soup.

**and then I'll have** _____ .

Waiter: And would you like something to drink?

You: **What soft drinks have you got?**

Waiter: Coke, orange juice, milk...

You: **I'll have** _____ **, please.**

Waiter: Bread and butter?

You: _____ .

## Take-aways

● 'A take-away' is a meal you buy to take home or eat outside.

● The most common kind of take-away meal is fish and chips. You can usually order:

**chips alone**

**fish alone**

**fish and chips together**

You will be asked whether you want 'salt and vinegar'. Some fish and chip shops still wrap your meal in newspaper. Others use special bags to keep it warm. Some give you a plastic fork.

● The following kinds of white fish are usually available

**cod      haddock      plaice**

Another kind of white fish called 'huss' is also available in certain parts of the country.

● Fish and chip shops also sell cooked pies and sausages.

● Other common kinds of take-aways are Indian and Chinese.

# 11 *Dinner at home*

It is difficult to give rules about the evening meal in a British home. It varies from family to family. One family will call it dinner and eat around 7pm. Another may call it tea and eat around 6pm. Dinner may consist of a three-course meal. Tea may consist of a cooked main course or a salad, plus a dessert.

## When you are offered food or drink

Would you like some ......?
▶ **Yes please.**
▶ **No thank you.**
▶ **No thank you, I'm fine.**
▶ **No thank you, I really couldn't manage any more.**

## Refusing something

Help yourself to the marzipan cake.
▶ **No thank you. I'm afraid I'm not very keen on marzipan.**
▶ **No thank you. I'm afraid marzipan doesn't agree with me.**
Avoid saying direct to your host **I don't like**.....

## Asking for more

| ▶ I wonder if I could have | another (piece of bread) | please. |
| | some more (milk) | |

## Saying you don't want much

| ▶ Well, yes please, | but only a small piece. |
| | but only a little. |

## When you do not want a large meal

▶ **Could I just have something light, please?**

# 11 *Dinner at home*

## Getting something you cannot reach

▶ **Could you pass the (bread), please.**

If you pass something to someone else, it is normal and perfectly polite to say nothing.

## Practice

Fill in the spaces in the following dialogue at dinner with your host. In some of the spaces, you have to say what you like or don't like:

You:    This meat is really lovely.

Host:   Oh, thank you. I'm glad you like it. I thought we would have something special for your first meal with us.

You:    _____ \_\_\_\_\_ . That was very nice of you.

Host:   Now, are there any things you don't like?

You:    Well, I'm not \_\_\_\_ \_\_\_\_ on \_\_\_\_\_ .

Host:   Oh, that's all right. We don't like it either. I was thinking of having fish or chicken tomorrow. Which would you prefer?

You:    Well, I think I'd rather have _____, please.

Host:   And later in the week I was thinking of making a curry. Do you like hot food?

You:    Well, to be honest, _____ _____ agree _____ .

Host:   Oh, that's a pity.

You:    Please don't mind me. You carry on and have curry and I'll just _____ _____ light.

*It doesn't really agree with me*

# 12 *Invitation to dinner*

## Information

- If you are invited to 'dinner,' expect a three-course meal.
- If you are invited for 'a little supper,' expect something lighter.
- "7 for 7.30", means drinks at 7 and meal at 7.30.

## Arriving

Hello. Nice to see you. Come on in.

▶ **Hello. How are you? I've brought you** a small present/a few flowers/some chocolates.

That's very kind of you. You shouldn't have bothered.

It is not normal to reply to this last remark.

## Starting the meal

Would you like to come through/ to the table now. I think everything's ready.

▶ **Thank you. Oh, this looks lovely.**

There is no phrase in English to translate *Bon appetit* !; *Guten appetit* !; *Que aproveche* ! and so on. In fact, your British host may use your language – if (s)he knows it!

## During the meal

It is polite to make a comment while you are eating.

▶ **This is lovely/ very nice/ absolutely delicious.**

Thank you. I'm glad you like it. Would you like some more?

▶ **Oh thank you. Just a little then, please.**

▶ **No, it really is lovely, but I don't think I could manage any more, thank you.**

## Coffee?

Coffee?

▶ **Black, please.**          ▶ **White for me, please.**

# 12 *Invitation to dinner*

## After the meal

▶ Thank you. | That was very nice.
| That was really lovely.
| That was lovely. I really enjoyed it.

## Leaving

It is very important at the end of an evening, that you do NOT just stand up and announce that you are leaving. If you do that, your British host will think that there is something wrong – perhaps (s)he has upset you. British people usually say at least twice that they are going to leave. There is usually at least ten minutes – or longer – between the two. You can say any of the following:

▶ **Goodness, is that the time!** | **I'll have to be going.**
| **I must be going soon.**

▶ **I really will have to go now.**

▶ **I really must go.**

Usually you use two different expressions – one the first time, one the second time. The ones with -**ing** are usually used first and the ones without - **ing** when you really are ready to go.

Here are a couple of useful phrases you may need before you leave:

▶ **May I call a taxi, please?**

▶ **May I just use the loo before I go?**

## Thanking

At the door:

▶ **Well, thank you again. It's been a lovely evening.**

A day or two later:

▶ **That was a very nice meal yesterday/the other day.**

# 13 *The Weather*

## Showing you are friendly

● In Britain friendly people start conversations by talking about the weather. Look at this example:

It's a lovely morning, isn't it.

▶ **Yes, beautiful, isn't it.**

Notice the answer agrees but uses a different word with the same meaning.

● Words for Good Weather

**Beautiful**
**Lovely**
**Wonderful**
**Marvellous**

Words for Bad Weather

**Awful**
**Terrible**
**Miserable**
**Dreadful**

● Do not just reply **Yes** or **No**.
Use a different word with the same meaning (see above).
Pass the conversation back to the other person:

▶ **Yes it is, isn't it.**

▶ **Yes it was, wasn't it.**

Add a comment about another day:

▶ **Yes** | **much better than yesterday, isn't it.**
| **warmer/cooler than yesterday, isn't it.**
| **I hope it keeps up, don't you?**
| **it makes a nice change, doesn't it.**

If you do not believe this, try it! You will be surprised how friendly people become when you start to talk to them.

# 13 *The Weather*

## Practice

Choose a remark from List 1, then the correct response from List 2.
Make sure you can say them naturally.

### List 1
1. It's a dreadful morning, isn't it.
2. I think it's clearing up.
3. Yesterday was awful, wasn't it.
4. This sun makes a nice change, doesn't it.
5. Lovely day, isn't it.
6. What a morning!

### List 2
a. Yes, terrible, wasn't it.
b. Yes, beautiful, isn't it.
c. Marvellous!
d. Yes, it does, doesn't it.
e. Yes, terrible, isn't it.
f. Well, things can only get better!

| | |
|---|---|
| 1 | |
| 2 | |
| 3 | |
| 4 | |
| 5 | |
| 6 | |

## Do you understand?

Pair up the natural expressions in List 1 with the meanings in List 2.

### List 1
1. It's clearing up.
2. It's clouding over.
3. It's drizzling.
4. It's pouring.
5. It's chilly.
6. It's sweltering.
7. It's rather sticky.

### List 2
a. It's hot and wet.
b. It's very hot.
c. It's raining very fast.
d. It's getting better.
e. It's getting worse.
f. It's raining a little.
g. It's rather cold.

| 1 | 2 | 3 | 4 | 5 | 6 | 7 |
|---|---|---|---|---|---|---|
| | | | | | | |

● You may hear these words. All of them mean *very hot*.
   **boiling**          **baking**          **roasting**

# 14 *In the street*

## Excuse me

Use **Excuse me** as your first words if you approach a stranger to ask something.

## Asking for help

▶ **Excuse me, have you the time, please?**

▶ **Excuse me, have you change for the phone, please?**

▶ **Excuse me, can you change a pound, please?**

▶ **Excuse me, can you tell me the way to (St Anne's), please?**

▶ **Excuse me, can you tell me if there's a (post office) near here, please?**

If someone asks you for help, they may begin:
Do you happen to know if...
I wonder if you could possibly tell me...
Sorry to trouble you, but could you...
I don't suppose you'd know if...

## At the bus stop

▶ **Excuse me, does the 44 go to (the station), please?**

▶ **Excuse me, does the 43 bus stop here, please?**

▶ **Excuse me, do you know if there's a 3A due, please?**
This means *Will a 3A come soon?*

▶ **Excuse me, which buses go to the sports centre, please?**

▶ **Excuse me, do you know if the (38/Highgrove) bus has gone?**

## Answering No

If someone asks you something, you do not just say **No**.
Excuse me, do you happen to know the time, please?

▶ **No, I'm afraid I don't.**

# 14 *In the street*

## Practice

Notice how the verb in the answer is linked to the question:

Have you got the time, please? ▶ I'm afraid I haven't.
Do you know the time, please? ▶ I'm afraid I don't.
Can you tell me the time, please? ▶ I'm afraid I can't.

Answer **No** to these questions:

1. Excuse me, do you know where Boots is, please? _____
2. Excuse me, have you a 20p coin, please? _____
3. Excuse me, can you tell me where Smiths is? _____
4. Excuse me, is there a telephone near here? _____
5. Excuse me, do you know this area well? _____
6. Excuse me, have you got a map? _____

## What's the question?

What question will you ask when you want:

1. the quickest way to the station

_____

2. a twenty pence coin for two tens

_____

3. somewhere that sells stamps

_____

4. the public library

_____

5. St. John's church hall

_____

6. the way in

_____

# 15 *Around Town*

## Project

You can learn a lot of English if you talk to people around town and keep your eyes open. Fill in the answers to this questionnaire about the town you are staying in.

1. Find names of streets which end in the following ways:

| | | |
|---|---|---|
| _____ **Road** | _____ **Street** | _____ **Drive** |
| _____ **Crescent** | _____ **Way** | _____ **Lane** |
| _____ **Avenue** | _____ **Square** | _____ **Close** |
| _____ **Gardens** | _____ **Terrace** | _____ **Place** |

2. Can you find street names which have the same name as:

Another British city _____ A British county _____

A British King _____ A British Queen _____

A flower _____ A British writer _____

3. What is the name of the biggest store in town?

_____

4. Most larger British towns have a branch of the following shops. Match up the shop with its description:

1. **Boots**              a. men's and women's clothes

2. **Woolworths**         b. modern design shop

3. **Marks & Spencers**   c. baby's clothes

4. **WH Smiths**          d. cheaper department store

5. **Next**               e. more 'up-market' store

6. **British Home Stores** f. less 'up-market' store

7. **Mothercare**         g. chemist and department store

8. **Habitat**            h. newsagent and bookshop

| 1 | 2 | 3 | 4 | 5 | 6 | 7 | 8 |
|---|---|---|---|---|---|---|---|
|   |   |   |   |   |   |   |   |

# 15 *Around Town*

5. What times are shops normally open during the day?

   _____

6. Write down the names of six places in town which every visitor 'must visit'.

   _____          _____

   _____          _____

   _____          _____

7. What are the names of the theatres in town? What kind of shows are on at the moment?

   _____

   _____

8. What are the names of the cinemas in town? What is the name of the main film at each this week?

   _____

   _____

9. Find the names of four churches in town.

   _____          _____

   _____          _____

10. Can you find out the names of any famous people who were born or who lived in the town? Sometimes there are plaques at the door of the house where they lived.

    _____

    _____

# 16 *Finding your way*

## Do you understand the prepositions?

| | | | |
|---|---|---|---|
| **on** | the corner | **at** | the traffic lights |
| **near** | the tower | **beside** | the cinema |
| **in front of** | the Town Hall | **next to** | the car park |
| **not far from** | the station | **opposite** | Woolworths |
| **across from** | the bus stop | **in** | the shopping centre |

## Practice

Use these prepositions to talk about the town where you are staying.

1. The station is _____
2. The post office is _____
3. The swimming pool is _____
4. The Town Hall is _____
5. The bus station is _____
6. Woolworths is _____
7. Marks & Spencers is _____
8. _____ is next to Woolworths.
9. _____ is opposite the station.
10. There's a _____ in the town centre.

## Asking your way

▶ **Excuse me, could you tell me** | where Victoria Road is, please?

if I'm anywhere near Station Road?

how to get to Station Road?

or simply,

▶ **Excuse me, I'm looking for Station Road, please.**

# 16 *Finding your way*

## Understanding directions

Study this conversation, then fill in the spaces in the summary:

**You:** Excuse me, am I anywhere near the Jubilee Sports Centre?

**Stranger:** Oh, goodness, no! You want the sports centre in Victoria Street, and you've come all the way to Victoria Road. It's very confusing, isn't it? No, you're miles away. You should be on the other side of town. What you want to do is go straight back down, right to the end of Victoria Road, where it joins Chelston Avenue. Then turn right and go along Chelston Avenue until you come to the Odeon cinema. There's a roundabout just after that. You want to turn left at the roundabout. Victoria Street is a couple of hundred yards down there to the right. And the place you want is a good 5 minute's walk from there.

**You:** So can I just check. I go _____ down Victoria Road as _____ as Chelston Avenue. Then I _____ and go as _____ as the Odeon. Then I _____ at the roundabout and then _____ after a couple of hundred yards.

**Stranger:** Yes, that's it.

**You:** Thank you very much.

*"Turn left at the red socks, then straight on until you come to the striped pants and turn right, then . . ."*

# 17 *Local Buses*

## Information

- In most towns there are different kinds of bus 'pass'. Each town has its own system for these tickets which will save you money if you have to use buses every day.

- Unlike your own country, in any British town there may be more than one bus company. The buses from the different companies may even run on the same routes.

- If you are waiting at a bus stop with the sign 'Request Stop', it means the bus will only stop if you stick your arm out to signal to the driver.

- When you get on to a bus, the driver or conductor will expect you to say your destination clearly. Say, for example: **Marina Drive, please** or **Two to the station, please.** On many buses where you pay the driver as you get on, you will see the sign:

> **Please tender correct fare**
> **and state your destination.**

## At the bus stop

▶ **Excuse me, do you know if** | the 15 stops here?
| the 12 runs on Sundays?
| the 44 goes past the pier?

▶ **Excuse me, do you know** | when the next number 12 is due?
| how often the 13A runs?

## If you don't know when to get off

▶ **Could you let me know where to get off for the swimming pool, please?**

# 17 *Local Buses*

## Practice

Match up the words in List 1 with their meanings in
List 2:

**List 1**
1. peak times
2. terminus
3. frequency
4. route taken
5. the operator
6. unlimited
7. zone
8. valid
9. fare
10. not transferable

**List 2**
a. the bus company
b. the way the bus goes
c. special area
d. the money you pay
e. only you can use it
f. end stop
g. how often buses run
h. without restriction
i. usable
j. rush hours

| 1 | |
|---|---|
| **2** | |
| **3** | |
| **4** | |
| **5** | |
| **6** | |
| **7** | |
| **8** | |
| **9** | |
| **10** | |

Now fill in the words from List 1 in the spaces:

If a bus pass is _____ , it means you cannot lend it
to a friend.

If your pass is only _____ within a particular _____ it
means you cannot use it outside that _____ .

If your pass allows you _____ travel, it means you can go
anywhere at any time.

## Find out

1. What are the names and colours of the different bus companies in
   the town you are staying?

   _____

2. What is the name in your town for a weekly bus pass?

   _____

3. Try to find out if there are any special tickets for old age
   pensioners.

   _____

# 18 *Going by train*

## Information

- **A single** is a one-way ticket.
- If you ask for **a return**, the clerk may ask you when you are coming back. This is because there are at least two types of return ticket:
  **An ordinary return** – the more expensive and valid on any train for a period of three months
  **A cheap day return** – valid only on the day you buy it, and usually only after a certain time in the morning. Check first!
- If you are staying in a town near London and you want a day return to London, you may be able to buy a rail ticket which is also valid on the London Underground.
- Always keep your ticket until the end of your journey, when your ticket may be collected at the barrier.

## At the Enquiry Office

- ► When's the next train to (Bournemouth), please?
- ► Is there anything a bit later/earlier, please?
- ► Is there a train to (Oxford) at about (9 o'clock), please?
- ► Is it the same service on Sundays?
- ► What time does it get to (Edinburgh), please?
- ► Is there a buffet/restaurant car on the 7.15, please?
- ► Which platform does the 8.13 go from, please?

## Practice

What questions will you ask about these:

1. Platform  – 8.37?
2. Buffet car – 12.07?
3. 13.20 – get in?
4. 16.00 – direct?
5. 17.09 – change?
6. 23.15 – sleeper?

1. _____
2. _____
3. _____
4. _____
5. _____
6. _____

# 18 *Going by train*

## Buying a ticket

▶ **A day return to London, please.**
▶ **A single to Birmingham, please.**
▶ **Two day returns to Oxford, please.**
▶ **An ordinary return to Cambridge, please.**
▶ **And which platform is it, please?**

## Speaking to another passenger

Remember, if you speak to a stranger, you usually begin **Excuse me**.

▶ **Is this seat taken?**
▶ **Are these two taken?**
▶ **Do you mind if I move your bag, please?**
▶ **Could you keep an eye on my things for a moment, please?**
▶ **Do you mind if I close/open the window, please?**
▶ **Is this (York) we're coming to?**
▶ **Do you know** | if there's a buffet car on the train?
| if we're on time?
| what time we get to (York)?

## Practice

Fill in the spaces in this conversation:

You:     A return to Victoria, _____ .
Clerk:   When are you coming back?
You:     Tonight.
Clerk:   And do you want an underground ticket as well?
You:     Yes _____ .
Clerk:   Then you want a Capitalcard. That'll be £8.40.
You:     _____ _____ ____ ____ .

# 19 *Time*

## Compare with your own country

Different countries have different ideas of the 'normal' times for doing things. Fill in the spaces below and see if your country and Britain are the same.

| | Usual time in your country | Usual time in Britain |
|---|---|---|
| The earliest time of day you could telephone someone | | about 08.30 |
| People get up | | 07.30-08.00 |
| People have breakfast | | about 08.00 |
| People start work in offices | | 09.00 |
| People have their "mid-day" meal | | 12.00 or 1 pm. |
| School starts | | 09.00 |
| Offices close | | 5.00 pm. |
| Most shops are open | | 09.00-5.30 |
| People have their evening meal | | about 6 pm |
| People go to bed | | about 11 pm. |
| The latest time of day you could telephone someone (who you do not know very well) | | 10 pm |
| TV closes down | | after 12 pm. |
| Latest time you could play a record player/radio in a block of flats | | 11 pm. |

# 19 *Time*

## Mealtimes

What does your host call the four meals of the day:

Morning _____   Mid-day _____

Early evening_____   Bed-time _____

In my family we have _____ at _____ , _____ at _____,

and _____ at _____ .

## Telling the time

● If the time is 12.17, you can say either:

► **It's twelve seventeen.**
► **It's seventeen minutes past twelve.**

Use **minutes** except with 5/10/20/25 past/to.

● Remember:  **It's half past two / a quarter past two.**
               **It's a quarter to two.**
               **It's four o'clock.**

● You will also hear the following:
   **It's nearly 4. It's getting on for 4. It's just before 4.**
   **It's just gone 5. It's just after 5.**
   **I'll see  you about six-ish.** (-ish means approximately)

## Practice

How many different ways can you say the following:

11.00   12.32   10.15   2.45   7.30   11.58   17.20

Use **-ish** to say when you normally do the following:

1. get up              2. get up on Sundays
3. leave home          4. get back home
5. have dinner         6. go to bed

1. _____   4. _____

2. _____   5. _____

3. _____   6. _____

# 20 *Money and Paying*

## Information

- British coins

  | 1p | 2p | 5p | 20p | 50p | £1 |

- British notes

  | £5 | £10 | £20 | £50 |

  The Scottish banks issue their own notes, including £1 notes. These can be used in England, but they cannot be changed outside Britain.

- Paying by credit card is very common in Britain, but check first if the shop takes your credit card. Please note that some shops only take their own credit card, for example, Marks & Spencers. Other shops have a minimum amount for payment by credit card.

- If you use your credit card for a large amount, you may be asked for identification or proof of identity. Your passport or driving licence should be all right.

## Getting change

▶ **Could you change a twenty pound note, please.**

▶ **Have you change for a twenty pound note, please.**

The cashier asks you:   How would you like it?
What would you like?

▶ **A ten and two fives, please.**

▶ **Four fives, please.**

▶ **Three fives and and the rest in coins, please.**

# 20 *Money and Paying*

## Paying in a shop

You can ask:  ▶ **May I pay by credit card?**
or
You might be   How are you paying?
asked:         Cash or credit card?

## If you have a student discount card

▶ **Do I get a discount with this card?**

## If you do not have change

When you only have a £10 note for something costing 45p!

▶ **I'm sorry this is all I've got.**
▶ **Can you change a £10 note?**

## How to avoid getting lots of change

When what you have bought costs, for example, £3.05.
▶ **I've got the 5p.**

## What do you say?

1. When you want to pay by VISA card.
2. When you want to change a £1 coin.
3. When you have a student discount card.
4. When all you have is a £20 note.
5. When you have spent £6.10.

# 21 Banks – Post Office

## Bank information

● Most British banks are open from 9.30am – 3.30pm Monday to Friday. Some of the larger banks in town centres stay open until 5pm. On Saturdays you will find some banks closed; some open in the morning; and some open until 3.30pm.

● The commonest banks are:
Barclays, The Midland, National Westminster, Lloyds and in Scotland, (and also in England): Bank of Scotland, Royal Bank of Scotland, Clydesdale Bank

● Building Societies are very similar to banks, but they do not have foreign exchange.

## Changing money

▶ **Could I change some** (francs, pesetas, lire), **please?**

▶ **I'd like to change** (10,000 pesetas), **please.**

## Travellers' cheques

▶ **Could I change some travellers' cheques, please?**

How much?

▶ **50 pounds, please.**

Could you sign them, please. And could I see some identification, please . . . your passport, perhaps?

## Credit cards

▶ **I'd like some money on my credit card, please?**

▶ **Could I use my credit card to get some money, please?**

## How would you like the money?

How much have you asked for in each example:

1. Could I have ten tens and four fives.     =     _____
2. Give me five twenties and five tens.     =     _____
3. Ten fives will do fine.     =     _____
4. Six tens, two fives and five £1 coins.     =     _____

# 21 Banks – Post Office

## Post Office Information

- Post offices are normally open 9.00 until 5.30 and on Saturdays until 12.30pm.

- As well as post offices, Britain has a system of 'sub post offices' – these are small shops with a postal department.

- You can buy stamps at any post office, sub post office and also in any other shop with a sign in its window which says that it sells stamps. Very often you can buy them in newsagents.

- Postcards and letters to EC countries cost the same as a 1st class letter in Britain.

## Buying stamps

▶ **How much is a letter to (Mexico), please?**

▶ **How much is a postcard to (Portugal), please?**

▶ **I'd like to send this airmail to (Chile), please?**

▶ **Could I have twelve twenty-four pence stamps, please?**

Write down how much it costs to send:
1. A first class letter in Britain.          _____
2. A second class letter in Britain.        _____
3. A 100g letter to your own country.       _____
4. A postcard to your own country.          _____

## Practice

What will you say when you want the stamps for:
1. 7 postcards to your own country          _____
2. 3 letters of 100g to your home           _____
3. 3 postcards and three 100g letters to your own country  _____

_____

# 22 Shopping

## Information

- Most shops in Britain are open from 9am – 6pm Monday to Saturday.
  In some small towns some shops close on Wednesday or Tuesday afternoons.
- Never put anything in your own bag or pocket before paying for it.

## Asking for something and pointing

| ▶ I'd like | one of those, please. |
|---|---|
| ▶ Could I have | some of those, please. |
| | a piece of that, please. |

## Asking for a particular thing

| ▶ I'd like | a can of coke, please. |
|---|---|
| ▶ Could I have | a Mars bar, please. |
| | a 35 mm slide film, please. |

## Practice

Can you match up the two lists of things you may want to buy:

| | | | |
|---|---|---|---|
| 1. | a packet of | a. | Ambre Solaire |
| 2. | a bar of | b. | milk |
| 3. | a bunch of | c. | chocolates |
| 4. | a box of | d. | rolls |
| 5. | a pint of | e. | soap |
| 6. | half a pound of | f. | roses |
| 7. | a quarter of | g. | matches |
| 8. | a tube of | h. | razorblades |
| 9. | half a dozen | i. | butter |
| 10. | a bottle of | j. | toothpaste |

| 1 | 2 | 3 | 4 | 5 | 6 | 7 | 8 | 9 | 10 |
|---|---|---|---|---|---|---|---|---|----|
|   |   |   |   |   |   |   |   |   |    |

# 22 *Shopping*

## Complaining in a shop

▶ **Excuse me, I'm sorry but I bought this** (pullover) **yesterday and it's too (big). Is it possible to change it?**
– Can I see your receipt?

▶ **Excuse me, I bought this** (camera) **yesterday, and it doesn't close properly.**
– Oh, you're right. I'm sorry. I'll give you a new one.
▶ **Thank you.**

▶ **There's a (button) missing.**
▶ **It doesn't work.**
▶ **It's scratched/torn/dirty.**
   Can you guess what the objects were?

## A very serious complaint

▶ **I wonder if I could speak to the manager, please.**

## Practice

Fill in the following in this dialogue: **Excuse me/please/I'm afraid/I'm sorry/thank you very much.**

You:          _____ _____, could you help me, _____?
Assistant: Yes?
You:          I'd like a film for my camera, but I'm not sure what kind.
Assistant: Can I see your camera?
You:          _____ _____ I've left it at home.
Assistant: Is it 35mm?
You:          _____ _____, but I don't really know.
Assistant: Does the film look like this or like this?
You:          Ah, it's like that one.
Assistant: Then it IS 35mm. Slides or prints?
You:          Prints,_____.
Assistant: 24 or 36?
You:          36,_____.
Assistant: That's £3.75, _____.
You:          _____ _____ _____ _____.

# 23 *Buying clothes*

## British sizes

- Shoes

| UK | 2 | 3 | 4 | 5 | 6 | 7 | 8 | 9 | 10 | 11 |
|---|---|---|---|---|---|---|---|---|---|---|
| Europe | 35 | 36 | 37 | 38 | 39 | 41 | 42 | 43 | 44 | 46 |

- Men's Shirts

| UK | 14 | 14½ | 15 | 15½ | 16 | 16½ | 17 |
|---|---|---|---|---|---|---|---|
| Europe | 36 | 37 | 38 | 39 | 41 | 42 | 43 |

- Men's Suits

| UK | 36 | 38 | 40 | 42 | 44 | 46 |
|---|---|---|---|---|---|---|
| Europe | 46 | 48 | 50 | 52 | 54 | 56 |

- Women's Dresses and Blouses

| UK | 8 | 10 | 12 | 14 | 16 | 18 |
|---|---|---|---|---|---|---|
| Europe | 36 | 38 | 40 | 42 | 44 | 46 |

Draw a ring round your own sizes in the above.

## Talking about your size

▶ **(man) My shoes are nines and I take a size 15 collar.**

▶ **(woman) I'm dress size 12 and I take size 5 shoes.**

You: _____

*"V-E-R-Y nice — it really suits you"*

# 23 Buying clothes

## When you need help

▶ Excuse me | can you help me, please?
| can I try this on?
| have you this in size 12?
| have you got this in red?
| have you this in medium?

## When you don't want help

Can I help you?
▶ **No thank you, I'm just looking.**

## When you don't want to buy anything

▶ **No thank you, I think I'll leave it.**

## When you don't know your size

▶ **I don't know my size.**
▶ **Can you measure me, please?**

## Paying

▶ **How much is this, please?**
▶ **How much are these, please?**

When you do not have change; for example, you only have a £10 note when something costs 80p: **Sorry I have nothing smaller.**

▶ **Do you take Visa/American Express?**
▶ **Do you take travellers' cheques?**

# 24 Using the phone

## Information

- There are two types of public telephone:
  - standard payphones which take coins
  - phonecard payphones which take phonecards
- You can buy phonecards from language schools, post offices, newsagents and other shops which show the green phonecard sign. The cheapest costs £1. The most expensive costs £20.

## Phoning your own country

- Calls abroad are cheaper on Saturday and Sunday and between 8pm and 8am on weekdays.
- In Britain you always dial all the numbers one after the other without waiting for a new tone.
- To phone abroad, dial:

| International | Country Code | Area Code | Person's number |
|---|---|---|---|
| 0 0 | (91) | without the first 0 (or 9) | 62106 |

- If you cannot pay for your call, dial 155 for the UK International Operator and ask to place a 'collect' or 'reverse charge' call.
- If you are calling abroad from your host family and you would like to pay them for a call abroad, you can ask the operator for an ADC call (advice of duration and charge) – the operator will connect you, then ring you back at the end of your call and tell you the cost.

## Phoning within Britain

- The cheapest times within the UK are all day Saturday and Sunday, and between 6pm and 8am on weekdays.
- Useful Numbers
  - **100** Operator
  - **155** International Operator
  - **192** UK Directory Enquiries
  - **153** International Directory Enquiries
  - **999** Fire, police, ambulance, coastguard

# 24 *Using the phone*

## Ringing the operator

▶ **Have you the code for** (Cambridge), **please?**
▶ **Have you the country code for** (Germany), **please?**
▶ **I'd like to make a reverse charge call to** (Norway), **please.**
▶ **I'd like to make an ADC call to** (Italy), **please.**

## Giving a number

0   = **oh** (not usually zero or nought)
63   = **six three** (not sixty three)
55   = **double five**
555 = **five double five**

## Practice

Say the following numbers:
**01273 736344**     **0171 568 703**
**00 33 1 477 039**     **00 58 2 884333**
Give your home phone number including the international code from the UK.

## Ringing a friend in Britain

▶ **Could I speak to** (Paul), **please?**
▶ **Is that** (669043), **please?**
▶ **Could you ask him/her to ring me, please?**
▶ **I'm sorry, I'm afraid I've got the wrong number.**

## Answering the phone

▶ **Just a minute, I'll get him/her.**
▶ **I'm afraid** (Mr Jones) **isn't here at the moment. Can I take a message?**
▶ **I think you've got the wrong number.**

# 25 Doctor and dentist

## Information

- If you want to see a doctor, you must ring first and make an appointment. If you want to see one quickly, you can go along to a surgery and wait. You can go to a hospital, but only if it is very serious and you cannot wait to see a doctor.
- Most countries have an agreement with Britain whereby it does not cost you to see a doctor. Check first!
- If you need medicine, the doctor will give you a prescription to take to a chemist's. There is a charge of a few pounds for each prescription.
- If you need to go to a dentist, you will have to pay for your treatment.

## In the chemist's

▶ **Have you got something for** | a cold, a cough, a sore throat, sunburn, a headache

## At the doctor's

▶ **I'm afraid** | I don't feel very well.
I've got | a bad stomach, a headache, a sore...
a pain in my...
my eyes, legs, are sore.
I've cut my ...
I've got a temperature.

## At the dentist's

▶ **I've got toothache. This is the one that hurts.**
▶ **I'm afraid a filling has come out.**

**Girls**
You may want to explain: *I'm all right thank you. It's only the time of the month.*

# 25 *Doctor and dentist*

## Parts of your body

Are you sure you know the words for each part of your body.
Translate the following into your own language. Check the ones you
don't know.

| | | | |
|---|---|---|---|
| head | ears | neck | forehead |
| wrist | shoulder | elbow | muscle |
| finger | thumb | chest | breast |
| stomach | back | bottom | thigh |
| knee | leg | ankle | heel |
| foot | toe | vein | heart |

SOMETHING
FOR A
HEADACHE!

## Patent medicines

You can buy some medicine direct from the chemist
without a prescription for minor problems.
Can you match up the problem and the medicine:

1. You've cut your finger.

2. You have a headache.

3. You have a sore throat.

4. Your nose is blocked up.

5. You want to clean a cut.

6. You have a bad stomach.

7. Your eyes hurt.

8. You have sunburn.

a. **Alka Seltzer**

b. **Calamine Lotion**

c. **Optrex**

d. **TCP**

e. **Throat Lozenges**

f. **Vick Inhaler**

g. **Elastoplast**

h. **Aspirin or Disprin**

| | |
|---|---|
| 1 | |
| 2 | |
| 3 | |
| 4 | |
| 5 | |
| 6 | |
| 7 | |
| 8 | |

# 26 Difficult situations

## Complaining in a shop

▶ I'm not very happy about this. I'd like to see the manager, please.

## Complaining in a restaurant

| ▶ I'm sorry but we | HAVE been waiting half an hour.<br>DID order 30 minutes ago.<br>asked for chips, not boiled potatoes. |

## If you lose your ticket

Can I see your ticket, please.
▶ I'm sorry, but I seem to have mislaid it...No, I can't seem to find it. I really am very sorry, but I definitely had it when I got on the train. Will I have to buy another?

I'm afraid so.

## You have forgotten your identification

Have you any identification?
▶ Yes, I should have my passport...Oh, I'm sorry I've left it at home.

Have you got a driving licence, student card?
▶ No, I'm afraid I've got nothing. Will this do? It's a letter from my language school.

Yes, that's fine. It's got your name and address.

# 26 *Difficult situations*

## If you are accused of something

1. Move your bag, please..it's in my way.
▶ **I'm sorry, but it isn't mine.**
2. Excuse me, but this is my seat.
▶ **Oh, sorry, let's check our tickets....Oh, I'm sorry but I think you're mistaken.**
3. Do you mind! You're standing on my foot!
▶ **Oh, I'm very sorry. I really am. I didn't realise. It's so crowded in here.**
4. Heh... that's my bag!
▶ **Oh, I'm very sorry. It's the same as mine. I really am sorry. There's mine over there.**
5. Heh...that's my bag!
▶ **I'm afraid it's mine. Look, my name's on it.**

## If someone is annoying you

If someone is annoying you, ask someone else to help you.
▶ **Excuse me, please help me. I'm a foreigner. This man/these people is/are annoying me.**
▶ **Please, go away.**
▶ **Please, leave me alone.**
▶ **If you don't go away, I'll call the police.**

## Swearing

If you try to use English swear words, you will probably sound silly. If you want someone to know that you are angry, it is best to do it in your own language!

# 27 A Day in London

## Advice

- If you are going to London for the day by train, try to buy a rail ticket that also includes travel on London buses and the underground. You will save a fortune on fares!

- If you do not need your passport and other valuables, leave them at home. Like every other big city, London has pickpockets. They work wherever there are crowds – especially on the underground. Wear a money belt!

- Try not to take £10 or £20 notes. It is safer to take £5 notes. Check your change in shops as soon as you are given it.

- Change money before you go to London. It will save time.

- Avoid "exchange bureaux" when you want to change money. A bank will probably be cheaper. Barclays, Lloyds, Midlands, National Westminster, Bank of Scotland, etc.

- If you want to know what shows are on, where, and how much tickets cost, buy a copy of **Time Out** magazine at the bookshop in the station where you arrive.

- If you want to buy a ticket to a play, concert, or show, ask about 'standby seats' or 'student standby seats'. These are cheaper but are usually only available on the day of the performance.

- Plan your visit to London before you arrive! If you don't, you will waste hours and risk being crushed in the crowds on the underground!

- London traffic is very busy. This can make taxis expensive.

- The tube is quicker than the bus, but you don't see as much!

- If you haven't got much money, take your own sandwiches and drink, as food can be quite expensive.

- You will have a very cheap day in London if you visit art galleries and museums. In Britain, they are usually free to everyone every day of the week.

- If you want to have a very frustrating day in London, join the queues at Madame Tussauds and the other most popular places. There is more to London than wax figures and Buckingham Palace! Good luck!

# 27 *A Day in London*

## London Puzzle

How well do you know London? Match up the clues on the left and the answers on the right.

| | |
|---|---|
| 1. Two squares | a. British |
| | b. Tate |
| 2. Two Crosses | c. Circle |
| | d. Trafalgar |
| 3. Two Art Galleries | e. Harrods |
| | f. Jubilee |
| 4. Two Railway Stations | g. Kings |
| | h. V and A |
| 5. Two Bridges | i. Bayswater |
| | j. Hyde |
| 6. Two big shops | k. Tottenham Court |
| | l. Tower |
| 7. Two Museums | m. Charing |
| | n. Regents |
| 8. Two Roads | o. Waterloo |
| | p. Leicester |
| 9. Two Parks | q. National |
| | r. Westminster |
| 10. Two Underground Lines | s. Selfridges |
| | t. Paddington |

| | |
|---|---|
| **1** | |
| **2** | |
| **3** | |
| **4** | |
| **5** | |
| **6** | |
| **7** | |
| **8** | |
| **9** | |
| **10** | |

Which street?

Which church?

# 28 The Tube

## Information

- There are 9 underground lines:

  | | | |
  |---|---|---|
  | **Bakerloo** | **Circle** | **Jubilee** |
  | **Northern** | **Victoria** | **Central** |
  | **District** | **Metropolitan** | **Piccadilly** |

- There are lots of stations where it is possible to change lines, so be sure you know your route! Check first on the map at the entrance to the station.

- The London underground is the oldest and busiest in the world. The platforms are much narrower and more crowded than many more modern underground systems. Be careful!

- If you come to London for the day from a town in the South-east of England, you can buy a special **Travelcard** which includes travel on buses and the 'tube' in the central zone.

- If you are already in London, you can buy a one-day Travelcard which allows you unlimited travel by bus, train, or tube in the greater London area.

- Remember that there is NO SMOKING anywhere on the London Underground – not even in the stations.

## Practice

The best way to get to know the Tube is to use it as much as possible. Use a map of the underground to complete the following:

1. Euston, Victoria, King's Cross, Paddington, Liverpool Street are all mainline railway stations on the _____ line.

2. If you want to go from Victoria to Oxford Circus, it's best to take the _____ line.

3. The nearest station to the British Museum is _____ which is on both the _____ line and the _____ line.

4. The _____ line goes all the way to Heathrow Airport.

# 28 The Tube

5. If you want to visit the Houses of Parliament, get off at _____ .

6. If you are going from Notting Hill Gate to Oxford Circus, take the _____ line.

7. If you arrive from Scotland at Euston, take the _____ line to get to Victoria!

8. The most direct way to get from Charing Cross to Bond Street is to take the _____ line.

9. Marble Arch is one of the busiest stops on the _____ line.

10. Piccadilly Circus is on both the _____ line and the _____ line.

11. If the Queen wanted to go home on the Tube, she could take the Victoria Line and get off either at _____ or at _____ .

12. If you are living in Wimbledon, you can get into town on the _____ line.

# 29 The Law and You

## How to avoid trouble

Most British towns are very safe places. But it makes sense to be realistic. If your passport or your camera are stolen, your stay in Britain will be ruined. We asked the police what advice they give to students on a language course. Here are their hints to help you enjoy your stay.

- In some towns there is a central meeting point where lots of language students meet. It is best not to stay there too long. Some locals can become annoyed by large groups of people taking over part of 'their' town!

- If you go to a disco, keep your valuables with you at all times. If you leave them at your table or underneath your chair while you dance, they might walk . . . .

- There are gangs in every country, so if you see a group of boys who look like a gang, it is best to ignore them.

- If someone buys you a drink in a pub or a disco, always be sure that you know what exactly is in it.

- Thieves find it easier to steal from people who have had too much to drink.

- Although the London Underground is very safe, there are pickpockets at work at all times.

- If you have been out late, try to walk home with a friend.

- Leave your passport and air ticket with your host family or in your hotel. In Britain it is very uncommon to be asked for identification.

- Take only enough money with you for one day at a time.

- If someone steals something from you, go to the police IMMEDIATELY. Do not leave it until the last day of your holiday.

These are practical tips based on the experience of the British police.

Remember! Britain is a very safe and friendly place. The British police are very friendly and will be pleased to help you.

**Ring 999 if you need the police fast! Have a good and safe stay!**

# 29 *The Law and You*

## At the police station

If you have to go to a police station, be prepared for lots of questions. Can you give all these details in English?

### Lost camera

1. What is your surname? What is your Christian name?
2. What is your date of birth?
3. Your address in (Hastings)? Your home address?
4. When did you arrive in Britain? When are you leaving?
5. Where did you lose your (camera)? When was it?
6. Was it insured? What's the name of the insurance company?
7. Does it belong to you? How much did it cost? What is it worth?
8. What make was it?
9. Can you describe it? What colour was it?
10. Does it have any special marks on it?

### Robbed

1. Whereabouts (where exactly) did the incident take place?
2. Were you alone? Were there any witnesses? Did you get their names and addresses?
3. When exactly did the incident happen?
4. Were you in any way injured? Have you been to a doctor?
5. What did the person take?
6. Can you describe your attacker? Male/female? How tall? Dark/fair hair? Colour of eyes?
7. What was s(he) wearing?
8. Did s(he) speak to you? Can you describe his/her accent?
9. What direction did s(he) run off in?
10. Did s(he) have a car? What make? Did you see the registration number?

# 30 *British Customs*

## Project 1

What is normal? Something which you think is normal, someone from another country may think is quite extraordinary. Here are some customs from different countries including Britain. Mark what is normal in your country and compare it with Britain.

|  | Usual in Britain | Usual in your country |
|---|---|---|
| Take your shoes off as soon as you enter someone's home | *No* | |
| Shake hands the first time you meet someone | *Yes* | |
| Shake hands when you meet a friend you last saw yesterday | *No* | |
| Kiss when you meet a friend you last met six months ago | *No* | |
| Kiss people on one cheek | *Yes* | |
| Kiss people on both cheeks | *No* | |
| Queue in a line if you are waiting for a bus or ticket | *Yes* | |
| Hold the door open for a woman if you are a man | *Yes* | |
| Touch someone several times during a conversation | *No* | |

Are there any other British customs which are different from your own?

# 30 *British Customs*

## Project 2

| | Usual in Britain | Usual in your country |
|---|---|---|
| Take a present if you are invited to visit someone for dinner | *Yes* | |
| Remove the paper from a bunch of flowers before you give them to someone | *No* | |
| Give flowers to a man | *No* | |
| Take a present of a bottle of wine for someone you do not know well | *Yes* | |
| Say thank you when you leave the table after a friend has given you a meal | *Yes* | |
| Write to say thank you when you get home after you have stayed with someone | *Yes* | |
| Arrive early for a party | *No* | |
| Arrive at exactly the time you were invited | *Yes* | |
| Arrive at a party one hour later than the time you were invited | *No* | |

Which British customs would you most like to change?

# 31 *Yes and No*

## Information

● It is very unusual to reply to a question in English with only **Yes** or **No**. It is more common to say a little more:

| | |
|---|---|
| Would you like another? | ▶ **Yes, please.** |
| Did you say half past? | ▶ **Yes, that's right.** |
| Did you go to the disco? | ▶ **No, I didn't. I was too tired.** |
| Can you stay for a drink? | ▶ **No, I'm afraid I can't. I've got to leave.** |

● If you use **Yes** and **No** alone, you will make yourself difficult to talk to. People may think that you are rude.

## Practice

Match these four answers to the questions:

        a. **Yes, please.**
        b. **Yes, that's right.**
        c. **Yes, certainly.**
        d. **Yes, thank you.**

1. May I have another cake?

2. Can I help you?

3. May I look at your timetable, please?

4. Would you like to come?

5. Are you feeling better now?

6. Did you say it costs £5?

7. May I use your phone?

8. Would you like a little more?

9. Can I get you a coffee?

10. Can I carry this for you?

# 31 Yes and No

## Practice

**No** on its own can sound very aggressive:

    a. Have you the time, please?    No!
    b. Would you like a cup of tea?    No!
    c. May I open this window?    No!

It would be better to reply:

    a. **No, I'm afraid not.**
    b. **No, thank you.**
    c. **I'd rather you didn't (if you don't mind).**

Match up these replies with the following questions:

1. Would you like another sandwich?
2. Do you know if this bus goes to the station?
3. Do you fancy something to eat?
4. Sugar?
5. Do you mind if I smoke?
6. Shall I get you a ticket?
7. Is the strike over yet?
8. May I watch the late night movie?

## Being Friendly

If a British friend asks you a question and you answer with only **Yes** or **No**, your friend will think you are "difficult to talk to". You should add an extra piece of information.

    Have you been here before?

▶   **Yes, I have. I was here last year.**

Match up the following questions and answers to make natural dialogues:

1. Have you been to London?    a. No, I couldn't afford to.
2. Did you like it?    b. No, I was with a friend.
3. Did you go to The Tower?    c. Yes I am...next Saturday.
4. Were you alone?    d. Yes, I have. Last weekend.
5. Did you go to the theatre?    e. Oh yes, very much!
6. Are you going again?    f. Yes, it was very interesting

| 1 | 2 | 3 | 4 | 5 | 6 |
|---|---|---|---|---|---|
|   |   |   |   |   |   |

# 32 Please

## Information

This is, perhaps, the most important word in English! If you don't use it when you ask for something you can easily upset people.

Use **please**:

● At the beginning of invitations    ▶ **Please come in.**

                                                  ▶ **Please take your coat off.**

● At the end of requests:                ▶ **Could you pass the sugar, please.**

                                                  ▶ **Four of those apples, please.**

● In the middle, with a heavy stress it often means the speaker is asking for the second time, or is slightly annoyed. You should usually avoid using it in the middle – unless you are annoyed!

## Please at the beginning

**Please** comes at the beginning of written notices. Use **please** at the beginning of these invitations. Make sure you sound helpful.

1. Start
2. Come in.
3. Help yourself.
4. Don't wait for me.
5. Take your time.

# 32 *Please*

## Asking with please

When you ask for things in shops, etc. say *only* what you want followed by **please.**

Ask for the following. Add **please** at the end of each one.

1. Single to London.
2. Day return to Brighton.
3. One of those peaches.
4. The Times.
5. Two of those.
6. A small piece of that.
7. Two halves of bitter.
8. Two nineties.

This means two 90 pence fares on, for example, the bus.

9. Two black coffees.
10. A cheese sandwich and a cup of tea.
11. Something for a headache.
12. Half a pound of these.

● **Please** is sometimes used on its own to mean *Yes, that's right* or *Yes, thank you.*

Did you say a cheese sandwich and a cup of tea?

▶ **Please.**

Would you like a cup?

▶ **Please.**

## Could I ... please?

If you are sitting down, for example in a restaurant, we normally say more than just ... **please.** In this situation we use:

▶ **Could I have .... please?**

Without the first phrase the request sounds rather aggressive.

Practise the phrase with:

1. The menu.
2. A knife.
3. A glass of water.
4. A roll.
5. Some more butter.
6. The bill.

# 33 Excuse me–Sorry

## Excuse me

● Use **Excuse me:**

1. *before* you disturb somebody, for example to get past.
   ▶ **Excuse me, could you tell me....**

2. to attract somebody's attention when you do not know their name:
   ▶ **Excuse me.... !**
   Say this loud and on a high pitch.

3. *after* you have sneezed, coughed, etc

## Sorry

● Use **Sorry:**
1. if you have slightly inconvenienced somebody.
2. with your voice going up at the end to ask someone to repeat what they said.

Here you can also use **Pardon?** or **I beg your pardon?** (but you cannot use **Excuse me** here).

Remember the basic rule for **Excuse me** and **Sorry** is:
**Excuse me** *before* we do something
**Sorry** *after* we have done something

## A more serious apology

● To apologise for something more serious, **sorry** on its own is not enough. Use:
▶ **I AM sorry**. (stress **am**)
▶ **I'm extremely sorry**.

● When you answer an apology for something small and unimportant, you say **sorry** too. For example, someone bumps into you:

They say:  **Sorry.**
You say:  **Sorry.**

● When you answer an apology for something more serious. For example, someone has said something which has hurt you:

They say:  **I AM sorry. I didn't realise.**
You say:  **That's quite all right**.

# 33 *Excuse me–Sorry*

## Practice

Can you open the window?

▶ **Excuse me, could you open the window please?**

Change the following in the same way:

1. Can you pass the salt?
2. Can you close the door?
3. Can you tell me where the ticket office is?
4. Can you hold this for a moment?
5. Can you change a pound?
6. Can you show me how to use this phone?
7. Can you tell me what 'inconvenient' means?

## Practice

Excuse me, could I/you.......?

▶ **Of course, I'm so sorry. I didn't realise.**

Practise making conversations. Sometimes you need **could I** and sometimes you need **could you.**

1. Get past.
2. Have the sugar.
3. Move your case.

4. Turn it down a little.
5. Put my bag there.

# 34 *I'm afraid*

## Information

- Everyone knows that you can say *I'm afraid of the dark/spiders*.
  **I'm afraid** has another very important meaning in conversation.
  It is the way to start to say something negative, for example:

  Have you got the time please? ► **I'm afraid I haven't.**

  Do you know the way?         ► **I'm afraid I don't.**

- This use of **I'm afraid** in conversation is much more common
  than its other meaning. Saying negative things can be difficult. It
  is much easier if you use **I'm afraid.**

## Practice

Match up the questions and answers:

| | |
|---|---|
| 1. Did you post my letter? | a. I'm afraid there isn't. |
| 2. Can you change a pound? | b. I'm afraid not. |
| 3. Does the 44 bus stop here? | c. I'm afraid I didn't. |
| 4. Is there a toilet here? | d. I'm afraid I can't. |
| 5. Are the banks closed? | e. I'm afraid it doesn't. |
| 6. Are you Jane Owen? | f. I'm afraid they are. |

| | |
|---|---|
| **1** | |
| **2** | |
| **3** | |
| **4** | |
| **5** | |
| **6** | |

Notice that the answer to number 5 was negative in meaning.

## Practice

What do you say?

1. When someone asks you for the time, but you have left your
   watch at home.

   _____

2. When a friend suggests you go out with him tonight, but you have
   promised to go out with someone else.

   _____

3. When a friend asks you for two twenty pence pieces, but you only
   have a five pound note.

   _____

4. When a friend asks you if you went to the concert last night, but
   there were no tickets left.

   _____

# 35 *Agreeing*

## So .... I

- One of the most important things you need to be able to do is to agree with someone. For example:

I love windsurfing.

▶ **So do I. Let's go and find out where we can hire a board.**

Look at the pattern:

| | |
|---|---|
| I can play tennis. | ▶ **So can I.** |
| I've just left school. | ▶ **So have I.** |
| I'm going to the beach. | ▶ **So am I.** |
| I love dancing. | ▶ **So do I.** |

- You repeat the auxiliary in the **So....I** part. If there is no auxiliary, use part of **(do)**.

## Practice

Match up the two parts of these conversations:

| | | |
|---|---|---|
| 1. I'm thinking of going to the beach. | a. **So could I.** | 1 |
| 2. I can play badminton. | b. **So would I.** | 2 |
| 3. I'd love to go to the play. | c. **So do I.** | 3 |
| 4. I could come early. | d. **So can I.** | 4 |
| 5. I like noisy places. | e. **So am I.** | 5 |

## Practice

What is the response in the following:

1. I'm going to get some fish and chips. _____

2. I think they're dreadful. _____

3. I love roller-skating. _____

4. I'd love to get out of here. _____

5. I can bring something to eat. _____

6. I could get the 7.30 train. _____

# 36 *Using Tags*

## Information

- Tags are the little phrases you hear at the end of sentences in spoken English: **...isn't it ...wasn't he ...won't you.**

- They are extremely important if you want your English to sound natural and friendly.

- Some sentences with a tag are questions – your voice goes up at the end:

  You know him, **don't you?** (I think you know him, but please confirm this.)

- The most common sentences with a tag are not questions – your voice goes down at the end:

  It's a lovely day, **isn't it.**
  Bill, you know John, **don't you.**

The tag in these sentences invites you to say more. It is a way of encouraging more conversation.

## Making tags

- The basic rules are very simple:
- Positive sentence > negative tag
- Negative sentence > positive tag
- Use the same auxiliary in the tag as in the main sentence.
- If there is no auxiliary, use part of **(do)**.

## Practice

Add tags to the following:

1. It's a lovely morning, _____.

2. It's nicer than yesterday, _____.

3. It isn't very warm, _____.

4. We could go for a walk, _____.

5. It was a fantastic concert, _____.

6. You went on the trip, _____.

7. It starts at 7.30, _____.

# 36 *Using Tags*

## Practice

Add the tags in this conversation:

A: What awful weather! It's dreadful, _____ .

B: Yes, it really is terrible.

A: Never mind, they say it's going to get better, _____ .

B: Do they?

A: Oh, yes. There's better weather on the way.

B: Well, I hope it comes soon.

A: You're going away this weekend, _____ .

B: Yes, I'm going up to York.

A: You normally drive there, _____ .

B: Yes, but I'm taking the train this time.

A: More comfortable, _____ .

B: Oh, much more.

A: You'll be able to get some work done, _____ .

B: Oh, I never take work away with me.

A: Don't you! I thought you were a workaholic!

Notice that the six tags in that conversation were not questions.
Each was inviting the other person to say more and continue the
conversation.

*"He isn't very keen on cars, is he."*

73

# 37 *Responding to tags*

## Information

● If you 'answer' a conversation tag as if it were a question, people will find you difficult to talk to. A conversation tag asks you to develop the conversation and say more about it.

● You can respond in different ways:

You can agree:               He's very rich, isn't he.

▶ **Yes, very.**

▶ **Yes, I suppose so.**

▶ **Yes, definitely.**

▶ **Yes, he certainly is.**

You can 'echo' the verb:    ▶ **Yes, he is, isn't he.**

You can add something new: ▶ **Yes, he's got two Rolls Royces.**

▶ **Yes, I've heard he's mega-rich.**

● In each of these ways you are keeping the conversation open. If you just answer **Yes,** you kill it!

## Natural Responses

Study these natural ways of responding to tags:

That was very disappointing, wasn't it.

▶ **Yes, I thought it was going to be much more interesting.**

That was very unexpected, wasn't it.

▶ **Yes, he seemed so young.**

You've just arrived, haven't you.

▶ **Yes, only a couple of minutes ago.**

He seemed a bit nervous, didn't he.

▶ **Yes, he did, didn't he. I wonder what was wrong.**

# 37 Responding to tags

## Practice

Add tags to these remarks. Then try to add an interesting response.

1. It's not a very nice morning, _____.
   ▶ _____

2. It's chilly this morning, _____.
   ▶ _____

3. You've done English at school, _____.
   ▶ _____

4. You've been here before, _____.
   ▶ _____

5. You're not an only child, _____.*
   ▶ _____

6. Wimbledon's on this evening, _____.
   ▶ _____

7. That's quite cheap, _____.
   ▶ _____

8. British people are very polite, _____.
   ▶ _____

9. British people do some funny things, _____.
   ▶ _____

*An 'only' child has no brothers or sisters.

# 38 Common Expressions

While you are in Britain, you will hear a lot of very common expressions which you may not have learned in school. Here are some of the most common. Try to guess the meaning of the expressions before looking at the answers.

## Practice 1

Match up the common expression in list 1 with its meaning in list 2.

1. What do you fancy?
2. Shall we go halves?
3. I'm only pulling your leg!
4. I'm starving.
5. I'm just going to the loo.
6. I don't follow.
7. I'm a bit hard up.
8. I'm up to my eyes.
9. You look knackered.
10. It was a rip-off.

a. very busy
b. very hungry
c. want to eat
d. very tired
e. no money left
f. cost too much
g. split the bill
h. joking
i. toilet
j. don't understand

| 1 | 2 | 3 | 4 | 5 | 6 | 7 | 8 | 9 | 10 |
|---|---|---|---|---|---|---|---|---|----|
|   |   |   |   |   |   |   |   |   |    |

## Practice 2

Each expression in list 1 means the same as an expression in list 2. Match them up.

1. Touch wood.
2. I'll just go a place.
3. You bet!
4. I'm ravenous.
5. I'm whacked.
6. I'm over the moon.

a. I'm dead beat.
b. I'm on top of the world.
c. I could eat a horse.
d. Definitely!
e. I'll just spend a penny.
f. Keep your fingers crossed.

| 1 | 2 | 3 | 4 | 5 | 6 |
|---|---|---|---|---|---|
|   |   |   |   |   |   |

# 38 Common Expressions

## Practice 3

Here are six expressions you could hear if you are staying with a family. Match them up with their meanings.

1. It's not my cup of tea.
2. I haven't got the hang of it yet.
3. I'm a bit on edge.
4. I'm really fed up.
5. I'm full up.
6. I'm a bit down today.

a. I've had enough to eat.
b. I'm a bit nervous.
c. I feel a bit depressed.
d. I don't like it.
e. I'm tired and irritated.
f. I can't do it.

| 1 | 2 | 3 | 4 | 5 | 6 |
|---|---|---|---|---|---|
|   |   |   |   |   |   |

## Practice 4

Match up the common questions in list 1 with their meanings.

1. What's the damage?
2. Do you get the point?
3. What's the catch?
4. What's up with you?
5. Do you get it?
6. What do you do?
7. What's the point?
8. Are you off?

a. Are you leaving?
b. Do you understand?
c. Do you understand the joke?
d. How much is it?
e. What is your job?
f. What's the problem?
g. What's the matter with you?
h. Why?

| 1 | 2 | 3 | 4 | 5 | 6 | 7 | 8 |
|---|---|---|---|---|---|---|---|
|   |   |   |   |   |   |   |   |

# Answers

**Page 9**  1. Is it alright to have a shower? 2. Can I walk to the school or should I take a bus? 3. Will I have my own key?

**Page 17**  Suggestions 1. Do you think I could have a shower...
2. I wonder if I could wash some shirts. 3. I wonder if I could ring...
4. I wonder if I could borrow... 5. Do you think I could borrow...
6. I'm very sorry but I've broken a glass. 7. Oh, by the way, I won't be in until quite late this evening. 8. I'm very sorry but I think I've broken the hot water tap...

**Page 19**  Suggestions 1. Watch out! There's a bug on your lettuce!
2. Thanks very much. 3. Thank you very much. I really enjoyed (this afternoon). 4. Would you excuse me, I'm very tired. 5. Excuse me a moment. 6. Can I give you a hand with the dishes? 7. Watch out! There's a plate under that paper! 8. Can I give you a hand in the garden?

**Page 21**  1d 2e 3a 4c 5b

**Page 25**  Suggestions You: Thank you. You: Well, I'm not very keen on (liver). You: Well, to be honest, curry doesn't agree with me. You: I'll just have something light.

**Page 29**  Practice: 1e 2f 3a 4d 5b 6c Do you understand: 1d 2e 3f 4c 5g 6b 7a

**Page 31**  Practice: 1. I'm afraid I don't. 2. I'm afraid I haven't.
3. I'm afraid I can't. 4. I'm afraid there isn't. 5. I'm afraid I don't.
6. I'm afraid I haven't. Suggested questions: 1. Excuse me, can you tell me the quickest way to the station, please? 2. Excuse me, have you two tens for a twenty, please? 3. Excuse me, can you tell me if there's a post office near here, please? 4. Excuse me, can you tell me the way to the public library please? 5. Excuse me, can you tell me how to get to St John's Church, please? 6. Excuse me, do know where the way in is, please?

**Page 32**  No 4: 1g 2d 3e 4h 5a 6f 7c 8b

**Page 35** I go straight back down Victoria Road as far as Chelston Avenue. Then I turn right and go as far as the Odeon. Then I turn left at the roundabout and then right after a couple of hundred yards.

**Page 37** 1j 2f 3g 4b 5a 6h 7c 8i 9d 10e, not transferable, valid, zone, zone, unlimited

**Page 38** Suggested questions: 1. Which platform does the 8.37 go from, please? 2. Is there a buffet car on the 12.07, please? 3. When does the 13.20 get in, please? 4. Is the 16.00 direct, please? 5. Do I have to change if I get the 17.09, please? 6. Is the 23.15 a sleeper, please?

**Page 39** please...please...thank you very much

**Page 43** Suggestions: 1. Do you take Visa? 2. Can you change £1? 3. Do I get a discount with this card? 4. I'm sorry this is all I've got. 5. I've got the 10p.

**Page 44** How much: 1. £120 2. £150 3. £50 4. £75

**Page 46** 1h 2e 3f 4g 5b 6i 7c 8j 9d 10a

**Page 47** Excuse me ... please ... I'm afraid ... I'm sorry ... please ... please ... please ... thank you very much.

**Page 53** 1g 2h 3e 4f 5d 6a 7c 8b

**Page 57** 1dp 2gm 3bq 4ot 5rl 6es 7ah 8ki 9jn 10cf, Downing Street, St Martin in the Fields.

**Page 58** 1. Circle 2. Victoria 3. Tottenham Court Road, Central, Northern 4. Piccadilly 5. Westminster 6. Central 7. Victoria 8. Jubilee 9. Central 10. Northern, Piccadilly 11. Green Park, Victoria 12. Central

**Page 64** 1c 2d 3c 4a 5d 6b 7c 8a 9a 10a/d

**Page 65** Practice: 1b 2a 3b 4b 5c 6b 7a 8c
Being Friendly: 1d 2e 3f 4b 5a 6c

**Page 69**  1. Excuse me, could I get past. 2. Excuse me, could I have the sugar. 3. Excuse me, could you move your case. 4. Excuse me, could you turn it down a little. 5. Excuse me, could I put my bag there.

**Page 70**  1c 2d 3e 4a 5f 6b
Suggested answers: 1. I'm afraid I don't have the time on me.
2. I'm afraid I can't. I'm already going out. 3. I'm afraid I don't have any change. 4. I'm afraid I couldn't get in/I'm afraid there were no tickets left.

**Page 71**  1e 2d 3b 4a 5c
1. So am I. 2. So do I. 3. So do I. 4. So would I. 5. So can I.
6. So could I.

**Page 72**  1. isn't it. 2. isn't it. 3. is it. 4. couldn't we. 5. wasn't it.
6. didn't you. 7. doesn't it.

**Page 73**  It's dreadful, isn't it...they say it's going to get better, don't they...You're going away this weekend, aren't you...You normally drive there, don't you...More comfortable, isn't it...you'll be able to get some work done, won't you.

**Page 75**  Suggestions: 1. It's not a very nice morning, is it. No, miserable, isn't it. 2. It's chilly this morning, isn't it. Yes, much colder than yesterday. 3. You've done English at school, haven't you. Yes, I did it for four years. 4. You've been here before, haven't you. Yes, last summer. 5. You're not an only child,, are you. As a matter of fact I am. 6. Wimbledon's on this evening, isn't it. Yes, shall we stay in and watch it? 7. That's quite cheap, isn't it. Yes, much cheaper than in France. 8. British people are very polite, aren't they. Do you really think so? 9. British people do some funny things, don't they. Yes, I saw a man yesterday....

**Page 76**  Practice 1: 1c 2g 3h 4b 5i 6j 7e 8a 9d 10f
Practice 2: If 2e 3d 4c 5a 6b

**Page 77**  Practice 3: Id 2f 3b 4e 5a 6c
Practice 4: Id 2b 3f 4g 5c 6e 7h 8a